From:

_____

Date:

_____

Message:

_____

_____

_____

THE PRAYER THAT *Changes Everything*®

BOOK OF PRAYERS

STORMIE OMARTIAN

HARVEST HOUSE PUBLISHERS

EUGENE, OREGON

THE PRAYER THAT CHANGES EVERYTHING is a registered trademark of The Hawkins Children's LLC. Harvest House Publishers, Inc., is the exclusive licensee of the federally registered trademark THE PRAYER THAT CHANGES EVERYTHING.

Cover by Koechel Peterson & Associates, Inc., Minneapolis, Minnesota

THE PRAYER THAT CHANGES EVERYTHING® BOOK OF PRAYERS
Copyright © 2005 by Stormie Omartian
Published by Harvest House Publishers
Eugene, Oregon 97402
www.harvesthousepublishers.com

ISBN-13: 978-0-7369-1411-6
ISBN-10: 0-7369-1411-0

Printed in the United States of America

05 06 07 08 09 10 11 12 /VP-KB/ 14 13 12 11 10 9 8 7

Introduction

If prayer is communicating with God, then the purest form of prayer is worship and praise. That's because it focuses our minds and hearts entirely away from ourselves and onto Him. Our worship and praise communicates pure love, devotion, reverence, and thankfulness to the Lord. It exalts Him for who He is. It communicates our longing for Him. It draws us close to Him. And when we worship God, we are the closes to Him we can possibly be. That's because praise welcomes His presence in our midst. In His presence is where we will find our greatest blessing.

Praise and worship should come naturally, but so often it doesn't. That's because we don't always know what to say or how to say it. It is my hope that the prayers of praise and worship in this book will give you words and thoughts that will be a starting point from which you move into powerful personal worship times. As you welcome His presence in your life with praise for all that He is and everything He has done, you will see changes happen in and around you like you have never seen before. That is the hidden power of praising God.

—Stormie Omartian

Give unto the LORD *the glory due to His name:*
Worship the LORD *in the beauty of holiness.*

Psalm 29:2

Because He Is
My Creator

O Lord, thank You that You created me and gave me life. "You formed my inward parts; You covered me in my mother's womb" (Psalm 139:13). I praise You, "for I am fearfully and wonderfully made; marvelous are Your works, and that my soul knows very well" (Psalm 139:14). I praise You that I was created for good things. Help me to be renewed in the image of You, my Creator (Colossians 3:10 NIV). I know You made me to be so much more than I am now and that You will help me become all You created me to be. Thank You, Jesus, that You are "the image of the invisible God, the firstborn over all creation" (Colossians 1:15).

Christ himself is the Creator who made everything in heaven and earth, the things we can see and the things we can't; the spirit world with its kings and kingdoms, its rulers and authorities; all were made by Christ for his own use and glory.

COLOSSIANS 1:16 TLB

Prayer Notes

You are a mighty God Creator of heaven + earth, Lord nothing is hidden from you Lord. You see all things, you know all things. Thank you Lord that you love me so much Lord that you took so great care in creating me. Lord thank you for continually looking after me and caring for me Lord in Jesus' name. I love ad most you Lord.

Because He Is
My Creator

Lord, I worship You as the Creator of heaven and earth. All things were made by You and everything You created is good. I praise You for all of Your beautiful creation. You placed the earth on its foundation so that it can never be moved (Psalm 104:5). Your right hand stretched out the heavens (Isaiah 48:13). Thank You that You have blessed us with light and dark, sun and rain, food and water, land and sea, trees and flowers, days and seasons. "The heavens are Yours, the earth also is Yours; the world and all its fullness, You have founded them" (Psalm 89:11). "How many are your works, O Lord! In wisdom you have made them all; the earth is full of your creatures" (Psalm 104:24 NIV).

———— ⁊ ————

Be exalted, O God, above the heavens; let Your glory be above all the earth.

PSALM 57:11

———— ⁊ ————

Prayer Notes

_____

_____

_____

_____

_____

_____

_____

_____

_____

_____

Because He Is My Heavenly Father

— ∽◈∾ —

Heavenly Father, I worship You this day. You are closer to me than an earthly father ever could be. Thank You that as my Father, You care about what happens to me. You provide for me, teach me, plan for my future, supply all my needs, and, because You love me, You will never let me get away with disobedience to Your rules. Thank You that "You have given me the heritage of those who fear Your name," and I have inherited great and eternal riches from You (Psalm 61:5). "LORD, you alone are my inheritance, my cup of blessing. You guard all that is mine. The land you have given me is a pleasant land. What a wonderful inheritance!" (Psalm 16:5-6 NLT).

Your Father knows the things you have need of before you ask Him.

MATTHEW 6:8

Prayer Notes

_____

_____

_____

_____

_____

_____

_____

_____

_____

_____

Because He Is My Heavenly Father

—— ∼❧∼ ——

Lord, help me to forgive my earthly father for anything he did or did not do. Show me if there is anything I have not forgiven that I am not seeing. As Your child, I long to make You proud. Help me to always do what is pleasing in Your sight. I want to be separate from all that would keep me separated from You (2 Corinthians 6:17-18). Thank You that I have been predestined to be adopted as Your child through Jesus because it gives You pleasure and it is Your will for my life (Ephesians 1:5). I praise and honor You as my Father God and give thanks always for all things, especially Your love (Ephesians 5:20).

———— ∽๏৴ ————

Seek the kingdom of God, and all these things shall be added to you. Do not fear, little flock, for it is your Father's good pleasure to give you the kingdom.

LUKE 12:31-32

———— ∽๏৴ ————

Prayer Notes

_____

_____

_____

_____

_____

_____

_____

_____

_____

Because He Loves Me

Lord, it is amazing that You love me so, even though I have done nothing to deserve it. "What is man, that You should exalt him, that You should set Your heart on him?" (Job 7:17). Thank You that You "see my ways and count all my steps" (Job 31:4). Thank You that Your "favor is for life" (Psalm 30:5). O Lord, "because Your lovingkindness is better than life, my lips shall praise You. Thus I will bless You while I live; I will lift up my hands in Your name" (Psalm 63:3-4). I love You with all my heart, mind, and soul, and I worship You as my God of love.

Can a woman forget her nursing child, and not have compassion on the son of her womb? Surely they may forget, yet I will not forget you. See, I have inscribed you on the palms of My hands.

ISAIAH 49:15-16

Prayer Notes

_____

_____

_____

_____

_____

_____

_____

_____

_____

Because He Loves Me

Lord, I worship You and thank You that You are the God of love. Thank You for loving me before I even knew You. I praise You especially for sacrificing Your only Son for me. There is no greater love than that. Your love brings healing to me for all the times and ways I have felt unloved in my life. I know that no matter what is happening in my life or what *will* happen in my life, Your love for me will never end. Because of Your love, "I will praise You, O LORD, with my whole heart; I will tell of all Your marvelous works. I will be glad and rejoice in You; I will sing praise to Your name, O Most High" (Psalm 9:1-2).

———— ❧ ————

In this is love, not that we loved God, but that He loved us and sent His Son to be the propitiation for our sins.

1 JOHN 4:10

———— ❧ ————

Prayer Notes

_____

_____

_____

_____

_____

_____

_____

_____

_____

_____

Because He Laid Down
His Life for Me

—— ❦ ——

Lord, I worship You and thank You that even before the creation of the world You chose me to be holy and blameless in Your sight. Thank You that because of Your great love, You predestined me to be adopted as Your child through Jesus in accordance with Your will. Thank You, Jesus, that because of You I have been redeemed through the shedding of Your blood. Lord, I know that I have sinned and fall far short of Your glory (Romans 3:23). Thank You for forgiving me. Thank You that even though I was dead in sin, You have made me alive in Christ (Ephesians 2:4-5). Thank You for the richness of Your mercy and grace which You have lavished on me.

For God so loved the world that He gave His only begotten Son, that whoever believes in Him should not perish but have everlasting life.

JOHN 3:16

Prayer Notes

_____

_____

_____

_____

_____

_____

_____

_____

_____

_____

Because He Laid Down His Life for Me

———— ❧ ————

L ord, thank You for sending Your Son, Jesus, to be my Savior and Redeemer. Praise You, Jesus, for the price You paid, the sacrifice You made, and the unthinkable suffering and death You willingly endured on the cross for me. Because of You, I am forgiven and now have made peace with my Creator. Thank You for giving me new birth into a life of hope because of Your resurrection. "You have also given me the shield of Your salvation; Your gentleness has made me great. You enlarged my path under me; so my feet did not slip" (2 Samuel 22:36-37). Lord, I thank You that I have been saved and reconciled to You because of Your Son, Jesus (Romans 5:10-11).

Blessed be the God and Father of our Lord Jesus Christ, who according to His abundant mercy has begotten us again to a living hope through the resurrection of Jesus Christ from the dead, to an inheritance incorruptible and undefiled and that does not fade away, reserved in heaven for you.

1 PETER 1:3-4

Prayer Notes

_____

_____

_____

_____

_____

_____

_____

_____

Because He Has Forgiven Me

Lord, thank You that You are continually willing to forgive me and mold me into a whole person. Thank You for convicting me of my sins so that I can come humbly before You and confess them. Thank You that no matter how far I stray from Your ways, You will always receive me back when I repent and cry out to You for forgiveness. Forgive me for my sins today. Remind me whenever I stray from Your laws so that I can confess and repent and receive Your forgiveness. I don't want any sin of mine to come between us. Cleanse me of all that is not of You. I worship You, O Lord, my Forgiver and Redeemer.

If we confess our sins, He is faithful and just to forgive us our sins and to cleanse us from all unrighteousness.

1 JOHN 1:9

Prayer Notes

_____

_____

_____

_____

_____

_____

_____

_____

_____

_____

_____

Because He Has Forgiven Me

—— ∽℘∾ ——

L ord, You are the keeper of my heart and the forgiver of my soul. I praise You for sending Your Son to die for me so that I could be forgiven. Thank You that You forgive my wickedness and will remember my sins no more (Hebrews 8:12 NIV). I know that I was dead in sins, but You, O God, have made me alive in Christ and have forgiven me of everything (Colossians 2:13). I am grateful that there is no condemnation for those of us who walk with Jesus (Romans 8:1). Thank You that the law of the Spirit of life has set me free from the law of sin and death (Romans 8:2). I praise You as my Lord and wonderful God of forgiveness.

Create in me a clean heart, O God, and renew a steadfast spirit within me.

PSALM 51:10

Prayer Notes

_____

_____

_____

_____

_____

_____

_____

_____

_____

_____

Because He Has Given
Me His Holy Spirit

—⁓∘⁓—

Lord, fill me afresh with Your Spirit this day. I let go of all else and open my life to all of You. Enable me to resist the temptations of the flesh that would cause me to stray from the path You have for me. I don't ever want to minimize all that You want to do in my life. Help me to be ever mindful of Your presence in me, and may I always hear Your clear leading. I want to show my love for You by embracing You with my worship and touching You with my praise. Teach me all I need to know about how to worship You in ways that are pleasing in Your sight.

_I will pray the Father, and He will give you
another Helper, that He may abide with you
forever._

JOHN 14:16

Prayer Notes

_____

_____

_____

_____

_____

_____

_____

_____

_____

Because He Has Given Me His Holy Spirit

―――⸚―――

Lord, I worship You and praise You and thank You for Your Holy Spirit in my life. Thank You, Jesus, for sending me the Comforter and Helper to teach and guide me every day. I praise You for the wisdom, revelation, and knowledge that You impart to me. I love You and the joy You bring into my life (1 Thessalonians 1:6). Thank You that I have been "sealed with the Holy Spirit of promise" (Ephesians 1:13). I know that I cannot understand the things of God in my flesh, but I can discern them in my spirit because of You dwelling in me. Thank You, Lord, for the gift of Your Holy Spirit in me.

Now hope does not disappoint, because the love of God has been poured out in our hearts by the Holy Spirit who was given to us.

ROMANS 5:5

Prayer Notes

_____

_____

_____

_____

_____

_____

_____

_____

_____

_____

Because He Gave
Me His Word

Lord, Your Word changes my heart, enriches my soul, and makes me wise. All Your commandments are true, right, pure, dependable, edifying, and life-giving, and that makes me glad. They instruct me, and I find great peace when I obey them (Psalm 19:7-11). Help me to hold "fast the word of life, so that I may rejoice in the day of Christ that I have not run in vain or labored in vain" (Philippians 2:16). "I will worship toward Your holy temple, and praise Your name for Your lovingkindness and Your truth; for You have magnified Your word above all Your name" (Psalm 138:2). Thank You that Your Word will stand forever because You, Lord, are the Living Word who always was and forever will be.

---⟨∽⟩---

The law of the LORD is perfect, converting the soul; the testimony of the LORD is sure, making wise the simple.

PSALM 19:7

---⟨∽⟩---

Prayer Notes

_____

_____

_____

_____

_____

_____

_____

_____

_____

_____

Because He Gave
Me His Word

Lord, I praise and thank You for Your Word. How I love that it gives me the guidance I need for my life. My delight is in Your law. Help me to meditate on it day and night (Psalm 1:2). "Your testimonies also are my delight and my counselors" (Psalm 119:24). Help me to fully understand all that I read in Your Word. Reveal everything I need to know. "Open my eyes, that I may see wondrous things from Your law" (Psalm 119:18). Thank You that every time I read Your Word, I know You better. Your Word is a love letter to me, showing me how much You love me. And every time I read it, I love You more.

———— ∽◉∾ ————

Great peace have those who love Your law, and nothing causes them to stumble.

PSALM 119:165

———— ∽◉∾ ————

Prayer Notes

_____

_____

_____

_____

_____

_____

_____

_____

_____

_____

Because He
Is a Good God

Lord, help me to trust that You are a good God no matter what is going on in my life. Help me to believe without any doubting that even if bad things are happening, Your goodness will reign in the midst of them all. Thank You that Your plans for me are for good. Thank You that the future You have for me is good. Thank You that You bring good things into my life. Reveal Your goodness to me more and more so that I may praise You for it. How great is Your goodness to those who trust and fear You (Psalm 31:19). O Lord, how excellent is Your name in all the earth (Psalm 8:1).

———— ⌇ ————

Oh, that men would give thanks to the LORD *for His goodness, and for His wonderful works to the children of men!*

PSALM 107:8

———— ⌇ ————

Prayer Notes

_____

_____

_____

_____

_____

_____

_____

_____

_____

_____

Because He
Is a Good God

Lord, I praise You for Your greatness and Your goodness. Thank You that You are a good God and Your mercy and grace toward me will endure forever (Psalm 118:1). May I never forget all the good You have done for me and how You have filled my life with good things. I desire, as David did, that I may dwell in Your house all the days of my life, to behold Your beauty and to be in Your temple (Psalm 27:4). I bless Your name, for You are good. Your mercy is everlasting, and Your truth endures to all generations (Psalm 100:4-5). You are my God and Lord, You are loving and patient, and You abound in goodness and truth (Exodus 34:6).

The LORD is good to those who wait for Him, to the soul who seeks Him.

LAMENTATIONS 3:25

Prayer Notes

_____

_____

_____

_____

_____

_____

_____

_____

_____

_____

Because He Is Holy

Lord, help me to be holy as You are holy. Establish my heart "holy and blameless" before You (Colossians 1:22). You who are mighty have done great things for me; holy is Your name (Luke 1:49). I exalt Your holy name above all names and will give praise and thanks to You every time I think of it (Psalm 30:4). Who does not reverence You, Lord, and glorify Your name? For only You are holy (Revelation 15:4). I give You the glory due Your name, and I worship You in the beauty of Your holiness (Psalm 29:2). "O Lord, You are my God. I will exalt You, and I will praise Your name, for You have done wonderful things" (Isaiah 25:1).

———— ✍ ————

Let them praise Your great and awesome name—He is holy…Exalt the LORD *our God, and worship at His footstool—He is holy.*

PSALM 99:3,5

———— ✍ ————

Prayer Notes

_____

_____

_____

_____

_____

_____

_____

_____

_____

_____

Because He Is Holy

—∽⊚∾—

Holy, holy, holy are You, Lord, and worthy to be praised. I worship You and thank You that You are perfect and lovely and pure and wonderful. The beauty of Your holiness is awesome beyond words. Thank You for wanting to impart Your holiness to me. Lord, I need Your holiness to penetrate my life and wash away anything that is unholy in me. Take away any attitude, any hidden sin of the mind, any activity or action that I do which is not what You would have for me. I know You did not call me to uncleanness, but to holiness (1 Thessalonians 4:7). Show me the way to holiness in my own life.

Give unto the LORD the glory due to His name;
worship the LORD in the beauty of holiness.

PSALM 29:2

Prayer Notes

_____

_____

_____

_____

_____

_____

_____

_____

_____

_____

Because He Is All-Powerful

Lord, You have said in Your Word that power belongs to You (Psalm 62:11). "Yours, O LORD, is the greatness, the power and the glory, the victory and the majesty; for all that is in heaven and in earth is Yours" (1 Chronicles 29:11). I know that by the power of Your Spirit, all things are possible. I give You thanks, "O Lord God Almighty, the One who is and who was and who is to come, because You have taken Your great power and reigned" (Revelation 11:17). "Be exalted, O LORD, in Your own strength!" (Psalm 21:13). I praise and exalt You as the all-powerful Lord of my life. Yours is the kingdom and the power and the glory forever (Matthew 6:13).

—— ∽☙∾ ——

Your faith should not be in the wisdom of men but in the power of God.

1 Corinthians 2:5

—— ∽☙∾ ——

Prayer Notes

_____

_____

_____

_____

_____

_____

_____

_____

_____

_____

Because He Is
All-Powerful

Lord, I praise Your holy name this day. You are Almighty God. You are the all-powerful, omnipotent Lord of heaven and earth. There is nothing too hard for You. Great are You, Lord, and mighty in power; Your understanding is infinite (Psalm 147:5). I know that because You can do anything, no plan or purpose of Yours for my life can be held back. "You have a mighty arm" (Psalm 89:13), and You rule by Your power (Psalm 65:6). You are the potter and I am the clay (Isaiah 64:8), and I give You full power over my life to mold me as You see fit. I surrender my life to You and release it into Your hands.

———— ∽☙∼ ————

Behold, I am the LORD, *the God of all flesh. Is there anything too hard for Me?*

JEREMIAH 32:27

———— ∽☙∼ ————

Prayer Notes

_____

_____

_____

_____

_____

_____

_____

_____

_____

_____

Because He Is
with Me

Lord, You are all I desire. Just being with You changes everything in me. Longing for You makes me long to be free of anything that would draw my attention away. I draw close to You this day. Thank You that You promise to draw close to me. With You I am never alone. I love Your holiness, Lord. I love Your beauty. With joy I draw water from the wells of Your salvation (Isaiah 12:3). Help me to make You the first place I run to when I have longings in my heart. I don't want to waste time turning to other things that will never satisfy the need I have for intimacy with You. My soul waits for You, Lord (Psalm 33:20).

I have loved you with an everlasting love; there-fore with lovingkindness I have drawn you.

JEREMIAH 31:3

Prayer Notes

_____

_____

_____

_____

_____

_____

_____

_____

_____

_____

Because He Is with Me

Lord, I worship You and praise You as Immanuel, my God who is with me. I long for more of You. I seek after You and thirst for You like water in a dry land. I want to stand under the gentle waterfall of Your Spirit and feel the soothing mist of Your love showering over me. I want to be immersed in the center of the flow of Your Spirit. I want to be close enough to You to feel Your heartbeat. You are the only answer to the emptiness I feel when I am not with You. The fullness of Your being is what I crave. The intimacy of Your embrace is what I long for.

Behold, the virgin shall be with child, and bear a Son, and they shall call His name Immanuel, which is translated "God with us."

MATTHEW 1:23

Prayer Notes

_____

_____

_____

_____

_____

_____

_____

_____

_____

_____

Because He Has a
Purpose for My Life

---∾∾---

Lord, I pray that You will reveal to me what I am to do and enable me to do it well. I don't want my own dreams and plans for the future to get in the way of what *You* have for me (Ecclesiastes 5:7). I know You desire mercy and knowing You more than sacrifice (Hosea 6:6). I long to know You more and to conform to the image of Your Son. May Your goodness, holiness, and beauty be upon me and establish the work of my hands (Psalm 90:17). Move me into the future You have for me as I walk in Your presence each day. Thank You that You created me with a purpose, and every time I worship You, I am fulfilling that purpose.

For we are His workmanship, created in Christ Jesus for good works, which God prepared beforehand that we should walk in them.

EPHESIANS 2:10

Prayer Notes

_____

_____

_____

_____

_____

_____

_____

_____

_____

_____

Because He Has a
Purpose for My Life

—— ～◌～ ——

Heavenly Father, I worship You as my Lord and King. I praise You that You are all-knowing and can see the end from the beginning. That You uphold all things by Your power. That You hold my life in Your hand. That You see my past and my future. I lift up to You all that I am and offer my life to You. Make me an instrument through which Your will is accomplished on earth. Use what I have for Your glory. Lift me up to see things from Your perspective, and help me to rise above my limitations. I don't want to limit what You can do *in* me and *through* me because I don't have an adequate vision of what Your heart desires to accomplish.

Therefore we also pray always for you that our God would count you worthy of this calling, and fulfill all the good pleasure of His goodness and the work of faith with power.

2 THESSALONIANS 1:11

Prayer Notes

_____

_____

_____

_____

_____

_____

_____

_____

_____

Because He Redeems
All Things

—— ✺ ——

Lord, I thank You for all the times You have redeemed my life from destruction. For all the times You have shown Your lovingkindness and tender mercies to me (Psalm 103:1-5). Everything in me blesses Your holy name, for You are the Lord, my Redeemer, who has made all things and made my life to be a testament to Your glory and redemption. You, O Lord, are my Father; my Redeemer from everlasting is Your name (Isaiah 63:16). "Let the words of my mouth and the meditation of my heart be acceptable in Your sight, O LORD, my strength and my Redeemer" (Psalm 19:14). I pray that You will continue to redeem my life in ways I never dreamed possible.

I know that my Redeemer lives.

JOB 19:25

Prayer Notes

_____

_____

_____

_____

_____

_____

_____

_____

_____

_____

_____

Because He Redeems
All Things

—— ❧ ——

Lord, I worship You as my God and Savior. I praise You, Jesus, as my precious Redeemer. Thank You for redeeming my soul from the pit of hell. Thank You for redeeming me from death (Hosea 13:14) and from the power of the grave (Psalm 49:15). Thank You for redeeming my life from oppression (Psalm 72:14). Thank You for love so great that You desire to restore my life in every way. Redeem me and revive me according to Your Word (Psalm 119:154). Thank You for Your goodness and mercy. "Draw near to my soul, and redeem it" (Psalm 69:18). "Redeem me and be merciful to me" (Psalm 26:11). Thank You for all the redemption You have already worked in my life.

———— ∽✆∼ ————

The LORD *redeems the soul of His servants, and none of those who trust in Him shall be condemned.*

PSALM 34:22

———— ∽✆∼ ————

Prayer Notes

_____

_____

_____

_____

_____

_____

_____

_____

_____

_____

Because He Is the Light
of the World

—— ◦◦◦ ——

Lord, thank You that I don't have to fear the darkness because even in dark times You are there. I know that "if one walks in the night, he stumbles, because the light is not in him" (John 11:10). But Your light is in me, Jesus, because You have come as a light into the world so that I don't have to live in darkness (John 12:46). The enemy wants me to dwell in darkness, but You have given me light. I choose to walk in that light. I need no other light but Yours. Whatever is good and perfect comes from You, the Creator of all light, and You will shine forever without change (James 1:17 TLB).

Arise, shine; for your light has come! And the glory of the LORD is risen upon you. For behold, the darkness shall cover the earth, and deep darkness the people; but the LORD will arise over you, and His glory will be seen upon you.

ISAIAH 60:1-2

Prayer Notes

_____

_____

_____

_____

_____

_____

_____

_____

Because He Is the Light of the World

———— ~∂☙~ ————

I praise You, Jesus, as the Light of the World. Your light is *in* me because *You* are *in* me, and nothing will ever change that. I know that You are light and in You is no darkness at all (1 John 1:5). "Send out Your light and Your truth! Let them lead me; let them bring me to Your holy hill" (Psalm 43:3). Lord, You see what is in the dark (Daniel 2:22). And when I am in darkness, You will be my light (Micah 7:8). I know that when I fall, You will lift me up again. I worship You as the Light of my life and thank You that You will enlighten the dark for me (Psalm 18:28).

But the path of the just is like the shining sun, that shines ever brighter unto the perfect day.

PROVERBS 4:18

Prayer Notes

_____

_____

_____

_____

_____

_____

_____

_____

_____

_____

Because He Is

Lord, You are holy and righteous, and I have no greater joy in life than entering into Your presence to exalt You with worship and praise. I will bless You at all times; Your praise shall continually be in my mouth (Psalm 34:1). I welcome Your presence now. And I thank You that because You *are*, I can *be* too. I will praise You, Lord, with all my heart, and I will tell everyone of Your greatness. You make me glad, and I rejoice in You (Psalm 9:1-2). I know that in Your presence I will find everything I will ever need. I know that when I worship You, it is the closest I can be to You this side of heaven.

Blessing and honor and glory and power be to Him who sits on the throne, and to the Lamb, forever and ever!

REVELATION 5:13

Prayer Notes

_____

_____

_____

_____

_____

_____

_____

_____

_____

_____

Because He Is

God, I worship You. I believe that You have always been and always will be Lord over everything. My soul longs for Your courts. My heart and my flesh cry out for You, the living God (Psalm 84:1-2). I long to know You in a deeper and more intimate way. My soul hungers to be close enough to You to feel Your heartbeat and sense Your love flowing into my being. I want to know everything there is to know about You. Fill my heart with such great knowledge of You that praising You becomes like the air I breathe. I want to show my love for You by embracing You with my worship. All honor, glory, and majesty belong to You.

Whoever offers praise glorifies Me; and to him who orders his conduct aright I will show the salvation of God.

PSALM 50:23

Prayer Notes

_____

_____

_____

_____

_____

_____

_____

_____

_____

_____

When I Am Troubled by Negative Thoughts and Emotions

—— ✒ ——

Lord, I praise You and thank You that You have given me a sound mind. I lay claim to that this day. Thank You that You are "not the author of confusion but of peace" (1 Corinthians 14:33). I choose peace this day, and I worship You, the God of peace. Thank You that I have the mind of Christ (1 Corinthians 2:16). Thank You that You enable me to cast down every argument and high thing that exalts itself against the knowledge of You and bring every thought into captivity to the obedience of Christ (2 Corinthians 10:5). Help me to be renewed in my mind and put on the new person You created me to be in righteousness and holiness (Ephesians 4:22-24).

If anyone is in Christ, he is a new creation; old things have passed away; behold, all things have become new.

2 CORINTHIANS 5:17

Prayer Notes

_____

_____

_____

_____

_____

_____

_____

_____

_____

_____

When I Am Troubled by Negative Thoughts and Emotions

---ى‍ى‍ى‍---

Lord, I worship You. You are my Lord and King, my precious Redeemer. There is no other God like You, entirely full of goodness, grace, and mercy. You heal us when we are broken-hearted and bandage our wounds. You build us up when we are weak in our soul (Psalm 147:1-4). You are great and powerful, O Lord, and You understand all things, even what is in my heart (Psalm 147:5). Thank You that I don't have to live with sadness, hurt, or depression. Thank You that "You have put gladness in my heart" (Psalm 4:7). This day I put on the garment of praise in exchange for the spirit of heaviness (Isaiah 61:1-3), and I glorify You as Lord of all.

You have turned for me my mourning into dancing; You have put off my sackcloth and clothed me with gladness, to the end that my glory may sing praise to You and not be silent. O LORD my God, I will give thanks to You forever.

PSALM 30:11-12

Prayer Notes

_____

_____

_____

_____

_____

_____

_____

_____

When I Have Anxiety, Fear, and Discouragement

— ✧ —

Lord, I give all of my anxiety and fear to You. I surrender my hold on them and release them into Your hands. I lift my eyes to You, for You are my help in time of trouble. I will praise You in the midst of all that happens in my life. I know that in Your presence I don't need to be anxious or afraid of anything. I refuse to entertain discouragement and instead choose this day to find my encouragement in You. Your love comforts me and takes away all my fear. Your power in my life gives me strength and makes me secure. Thank You for giving me the courage to go forward and fulfill the destiny You have for me.

This poor man cried out, and the LORD *heard him, and saved him out of all his troubles. The angel of the* LORD *encamps all around those who fear Him, and delivers them.*

PSALM 34:6-7

Prayer Notes

_____

_____

_____

_____

_____

_____

_____

_____

_____

When I Have Anxiety, Fear, and Discouragement

———— ❧ ————

O Lord, I worship You above all else. You are my light and my salvation; whom shall I fear? You, Lord, are the strength of my life; of whom shall I be afraid? (Psalm 27:1). I thank You that "though an army may encamp against me, my heart shall not fear" (Psalm 27:3). In You, Lord, "I have put my trust; I will not be afraid. What can man do to me?" (Psalm 56:11). "Whenever I am afraid, I will trust in You" (Psalm 56:3). Thank You, Lord, that when I seek You, You hear me and deliver me from all my fears, that You save me out of all my troubles. Thank You that Your angel camps around me to deliver me (Psalm 34:4-7).

I cried to the LORD with my voice, and He heard me from His holy hill. I lay down and slept; I awoke, for the LORD sustained me. I will not be afraid of ten thousands of people who have set themselves against me all around.

PSALM 3:4-6

Prayer Notes

_____

_____

_____

_____

_____

_____

_____

_____

_____

When I Become Sick, Weak, or Injured

———— ✦ ————

Lord, I lift up to You my affliction this day (name it before the Lord), and I ask You to take it away. I thank You for Your grace and mercy toward me. "I will extol You, O LORD, for You have lifted me up…O LORD my God, I cried out to You, and You healed me" (Psalm 30:1-2). "Bless the LORD, O my soul, and forget not all His benefits: who forgives all your iniquities, who heals all your diseases" (Psalm 103:2-3). Should You decide not to heal me in the way and time I desire, I trust that You will bring good out of my suffering and that it will glorify You.

*Heal me, O L*ORD*, and I shall be healed; save me, and I shall be saved, for You are my praise.*

JEREMIAH 17:14

Prayer Notes

_____

_____

_____

_____

_____

_____

_____

_____

_____

_____

When I Become Sick, Weak, or Injured

I praise You, Jesus. I exalt and thank You that You are my Healer. Thank You for dying for me on the cross, for bearing the consequences of my sin in Your body. You are greater than anything I face or suffer, and I thank You that in Your name I can find healing. Your power is unlimited. I know that if You heal me, I will be healed completely. Thank You that You will rise up with healing for those who fear Your name (Malachi 4:2). "Be merciful to me, O God, be merciful to me! For my soul trusts in You; and in the shadow of Your wings I will make my refuge, until these calamities have passed by" (Psalm 57:1).

He sent His word and healed them, and delivered them from their destructions.

PSALM 107:20

Prayer Notes

_____

_____

_____

_____

_____

_____

_____

_____

_____

_____

When I Struggle
with Doubt

Lord, it is by faith we stand (2 Corinthians 1:24). I want to have so much faith that I am fully convinced that whatever You have promised to me, You will also be able to perform it in my life (Romans 4:21). I know that faith is a gift from You, and I pray that my faith, no matter how it is tested by fire, will glorify You and bring all the praise and honor and glory that belong to You. Thank You that You have given me Your Word whereby my faith can be increased. Help me to grow in my understanding of it. May Your Word be so mixed with my faith that it will glorify You (Hebrews 4:2).

———— ∽☙∾ ————

Now faith is the substance of things hoped for, the evidence of things not seen.

HEBREWS 11:1

———— ∽☙∾ ————

Prayer Notes

_____

_____

_____

_____

_____

_____

_____

_____

_____

_____

When I Struggle
with Doubt

─────── ✐ ───────

I worship You, Almighty God, and give You all the glory that is due Your name. I praise You, Lord of heaven and earth, and thank You that with You all things are possible. The things that are impossible with men are possible with You (Luke 18:27). Thank You that You give faith as a gift to those who ask. Because of You, I don't have to live in doubt. I ask You to increase my faith to believe for bigger and greater things. Help me to always "ask in faith, with no doubting." May I never be like a wave of the sea driven and tossed by the wind because I have doubt (James 1:6-8).

In this you greatly rejoice, though now for a little while, if need be, you have been grieved by various trials, that the genuineness of your faith, being much more precious than gold that perishes, though it is tested by fire, may be found to praise, honor, and glory at the revelation of Jesus Christ.

1 PETER 1:6-7

Prayer Notes

_____

_____

_____

_____

_____

_____

_____

_____

When I Don't See Answers to My Prayers

———— ❧ ————

Lord, I know that what I may see as unanswered prayer may not be unanswered at all. It means that You are answering according to Your will. Whether I understand Your will or not doesn't affect the fact that I trust it and praise You for it. Thank You for Your unfailing Word and that You always keep Your promises to me. I thank You that Your power is infinite. Your judgments and Your will are perfect, and I trust them. Whether or not my prayers are answered the way I pray them, I will praise and worship You above all things. For You are my Wonderful Counselor, my Everlasting Father, my Stronghold in the Day of Trouble, and my Resting Place. I rest in You today.

Do not throw away your confidence; it will be richly rewarded. You need to persevere so that when you have done the will of God, you will receive what he has promised.

HEBREWS 10:35-36 NIV

Prayer Notes

_____

_____

_____

_____

_____

_____

_____

_____

_____

_____

When I Don't See Answers to My Prayers

———— ❧ ————

Lord, I worship and praise You as the all-knowing and all-powerful God of the universe. You are Immanuel, God with us. Thank You that You are always with me. Thank You that Your presence frees me from all doubt and gives me increased faith. Thank You that You hear my prayers and will answer in Your time and in Your way. You, Lord, are without limitations. I don't want to limit Your working in my life by my own faithlessness. Help me to "be joyful in hope, patient in affliction, faithful in prayer" (Romans 12:12 NIV). I know that You have called me to pray, but I also know that answering prayers is Your job. Help my heart to rest in You.

———— ◦ᥫ᭡◦ ————

Continue earnestly in prayer, being vigilant in it with thanksgiving.

COLOSSIANS 4:2

———— ◦ᥫ᭡◦ ————

Prayer Notes

_____

_____

_____

_____

_____

_____

_____

_____

_____

_____

_____

When I Have Problems in a Relationship

———— ✎ ————

Lord, I praise You as the God of restoration, for I know You can restore my relationships to complete wholeness. Help me to be in unity with others and to be compassionate, loving, tenderhearted, and courteous, "not returning evil for evil," but rather only giving blessings to them (1 Peter 3:8-9). I praise You as my Creator and recognize that You created all the people with whom I am in relationship. You are their heavenly Father just as You are mine. They are my brothers and sisters, and You love and forgive them as You love and forgive me. You laid down Your life for them as You laid it down for me. Help me to love them as You love me.

Since you have purified your souls in obeying the truth through the Spirit in sincere love of the brethren, love one another fervently with a pure heart.

1 PETER 1:22

Prayer Notes

When I Have Problems in a Relationship

———— ∾⊘∾ ————

Lord, I worship You. I praise You, precious God of love, and thank You that You have poured out Your love on me. I lift my heart to You and ask You to fill it so full of Your unfailing and unconditional love that it overflows onto others. Thank You, Lord, that You are the God who makes all things new, even our relationships. You can put new love in our heart. You can revive love that has died and make love live again. I give all of my relationships to You and thank You for them. For those who are closest and most important to me, and those who are most challenging and difficult, enable me to love them the way You do.

———— ❧ ————

A new commandment I give to you, that you love one another; as I have loved you, that you also love one another.

JOHN 13:34

———— ❧ ————

Prayer Notes

_____

_____

_____

_____

_____

_____

_____

_____

_____

_____

When I Need to Forgive

It amazes me, Lord, that You love me so much that You would sacrifice Yourself so I could be forgiven completely. "Your unfailing love is better to me than life itself; how I praise you! I will honor you as long as I live, lifting up my hands to you in prayer. You satisfy me more than the richest of foods. I will praise you with songs of joy" (Psalm 63:3-5 NLT). Thank You that You loved me, even though You have seen me at my worst. I praise You, heavenly Father, who is rich in mercy and grace toward me. Thank You that Your love and mercy are everlasting. Help me to become the loving and forgiving person You want me to be.

*Be kind to one another, tenderhearted, forgiving
one another, just as God in Christ forgave you.*

EPHESIANS 4:32

Prayer Notes

_____

_____

_____

_____

_____

_____

_____

_____

_____

_____

When I Need to Forgive

Lord, I worship You for who You are. I praise You, my precious and loving God of forgiveness. Thank You for forgiving me. Where would I be without You setting me free from the consequences of my own sin? Lord, I surrender to You everything that is in my heart. I want to be forgiving so I will always be forgiven (Matthew 6:14-15). Take away anything that separates me from You and hinders my knowing You better. Pour out Your Spirit upon me in a fresh new way and reveal anything in me that is not of You. Shine Your light into the corners of my heart and reveal any unforgiveness I have in me toward anyone.

---⟋∾⟍---

The discretion of a man makes him slow to anger, and his glory is to overlook a transgression.

PROVERBS 19:11

---⟋∾⟍---

Prayer Notes

_____

_____

_____

_____

_____

_____

_____

_____

_____

_____

When I See Things Going Wrong and I Feel Powerless

———— ∽∾∽ ————

Lord, as I go through tough times when everything seems to be going wrong, I draw near to You and disengage from the concerns of this life. I thank You that You are able to do exceedingly abundantly above all that I ask or think, according to Your power that works in me (Ephesians 3:20). I worship You, God of grace, and thank You that after I have suffered a while, You will perfect, establish, strengthen, and settle me (1 Peter 5:10-11). I praise You for Your power and thank You that You pour power into my life in great measure. I worship You, Father of mercy and comfort, and thank You that You comfort me in my times of trial.

My brethren, count it all joy when you fall into various trials, knowing that the testing of your faith produces patience. But let patience have its perfect work, that you may be perfect and complete, lacking nothing.

JAMES 1:2-4

Prayer Notes

_____

_____

_____

_____

_____

_____

_____

_____

When I See Things Going Wrong and I Feel Powerless

—— ❧ ——

Lord, I praise Your name. I exalt You above all things. You are my King and Lord. In the midst of everything that is happening in my life and all that I am going through, I know that You are the all-powerful God of the universe. Hide me in Your secret place in my time of struggle. Lift me high upon a rock so that I may rise above the plans of my enemies to surround me with problems. I will sing and offer You the sacrifice of praise (Psalm 27:5-6). You are my help, and I will hide myself in You. I praise You for all that You are. "My soul follows close behind You; Your right hand upholds me" (Psalm 63:8).

Beloved, do not think it strange concerning the fiery trial which is to try you, as though some strange thing happened to you; but rejoice to the extent that you partake of Christ's sufferings, that when His glory is revealed, you may also be glad with exceeding joy.

1 PETER 4:12-13

Prayer Notes

When I Long to Know God's Will

—— ✺ ——

Lord, I worship You and praise You as the all-knowing and all-wise God of the universe. All things are known by You. You know all of my days, and You know the way I should go. Thank You that You give wisdom to those who ask for it. And I ask for wisdom today. I know that having mere knowledge apart from You will never be enough to satisfy the longing in my heart. I can never know enough. What I need to know only You can teach me. Lord, I know it is Your will for me to give thanks *in* all things, so I thank You this day *for* everything You have done in my life (1 Thessalonians 5:18).

For this reason we also, since the day we heard it, do not cease to pray for you, and to ask that you may be filled with the knowledge of His will in all wisdom and spiritual understanding; that you may walk worthy of the Lord, fully pleasing Him, being fruitful in every good work and increasing in the knowledge of God.

COLOSSIANS 1:9-10

Prayer Notes

_____

_____

_____

_____

_____

_____

_____

_____

When I Long to Know God's Will

—— ∽∾ ——

Lord, thank You for giving me knowledge of Your will in all wisdom and spiritual understanding (Colossians 1:9). Thank You for guiding me and leading me. Thank You for giving me understanding from Your Word and directing my steps so I can stay on the path You have for me. Thank You for revealing to me the way in which I should go regarding every decision I make. I praise You for Your wisdom and knowledge and revelation. Thank You for helping me to stand perfect and complete in the center of Your will (Colossians 4:12). Give me the endurance I need, so that after I have done Your will, I will receive the promise (Hebrews 10:36).

He who does the will of God abides forever.

1 JOHN 2:17

Prayer Notes

_____

_____

_____

_____

_____

_____

_____

_____

_____

_____

When I Seek Breakthrough, Deliverance, or Transformation

— ❧ —

Heavenly Father, thank You that You have delivered me out of the enemy's hand. I know You will continue to deliver me until the day I go to be with You. I call upon Your name, Lord. "I implore You, deliver my soul" (Psalm 116:4). I know You have begun a good work in me and You will complete it (Philippians 1:6). I know that in whatever state I am, I can be content because You will not leave me there forever (Philippians 4:11). I will praise You in the midst of any need I have for breakthrough, deliverance, or transformation, knowing that You see my need and will meet it in Your way and in Your time.

Do not remember the former things, nor consider the things of old. Behold, I will do a new thing, now it shall spring forth; shall you not know it? I will even make a road in the wilderness and rivers in the desert.

ISAIAH 43:18-19

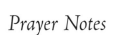

Prayer Notes

_____

_____

_____

_____

_____

_____

_____

_____

When I Seek Breakthrough, Deliverance, or Transformation

————— ❧ —————

I worship You, Lord. You are my rock, my fortress, my deliverer, my strength in whom I trust, my shield, my stronghold, and my salvation (Psalm 18:2). You looked down from above and "drew me out of many waters" (Psalm 18:16). You have brought me into a broad place and You have delivered me because You delighted in me (Psalm 18:19). You are my God and I will praise You (Exodus 15:2). Lord, I praise You as my Almighty Deliverer. You have the power to set me free and transform my life. Thank You that You will break down every stronghold that the enemy of my soul has erected in and around me. You will break down every wall that separates me from all You have for me.

The Lord will deliver me from every evil work and preserve me for His heavenly kingdom. To Him be glory forever and ever.

2 TIMOTHY 4:18

Prayer Notes

When I Need God's Provision and Protection

———— ❧ ————

I love You, Lord. I know that Your provision and protection are evidence of Your great love for me. I will call upon You, for You are worthy to be praised, and I will be saved from my enemies (Psalm 18:3). My heart rejoices in You. I trust in Your holy name (Psalm 33:21). I rejoice in You, I trust in You, I shout for joy because You defend me. Thank You that You bless and surround me like a shield (Psalm 5:11-12). You are my God, and I am one of Your sheep for whom You extend Your hand of protection (Psalm 95:6-7). You are my refuge and my strength in the day of trouble, and I will sing Your praises forever (Psalm 59:16-17).

The LORD is my strength and my shield; my heart trusted in Him, and I am helped; therefore my heart greatly rejoices, and with my song I will praise Him.

PSALM 28:7

Prayer Notes

_____

_____

_____

_____

_____

_____

_____

_____

_____

_____

When I Need God's Provision and Protection

― ∽◦∾ ―

L ord, You are King and Lord over all my life. I surrender everything I have to You because I recognize that every good thing I have has been given to me by You as a sign of Your goodness, mercy, and love (James 1:17). Thank You that You are my Provider and You provide everything I need. Lord, I praise You as my Protector. Thank You for hiding me under "the shadow of Your wings, from the wicked who oppress me, from my deadly enemies who surround me" (Psalm 17:8-9). "I will render praises to You, for You have delivered my soul from death. Have You not kept my feet from falling, that I may walk before God in the light of the living?" (Psalm 56:12-13).

Those who seek the LORD *shall not lack any good thing.*

PSALM 34:10

Prayer Notes

_____

_____

_____

_____

_____

_____

_____

_____

_____

_____

_____

When I Fight Temptation to Walk in the Flesh

———— ❧ ————

Lord, when I am tempted, show me what it is that is drawing me away from You. I praise You in the midst of any temptation I am facing, knowing You have the power to break its hold on me. Help me to "walk in the Spirit" so that I will "not fulfill the lust of the flesh" (Galatians 5:16). Lord, I know that "it is no longer I who live, but Christ lives in me; and the life which I now live in the flesh I live by faith" (Galatians 2:20). Create in me a clean heart and renew a right spirit within me (Psalm 51:10) so that I can worship You with a pure heart.

———— ∽◎∼ ————

For we do not have a High Priest who cannot sympathize with our weaknesses, but was in all points tempted as we are, yet without sin.

HEBREWS 4:15

———— ∽◎∼ ————

Prayer Notes

_____

_____

_____

_____

_____

_____

_____

_____

_____

_____

_____

When I Fight Temptation to Walk in the Flesh

—— ✺ ——

Lord, I worship You as my Lord and Savior. I praise You, Holy Spirit, that You live in me and enable me to move in the Spirit and not the flesh. I confess all my sins before You and repent of them. Specifically I confess (tell God anything you feel you need to confess). I don't want any sin in my life. God, help me to trust Your ways and love Your laws enough to always obey them. Help me to have such faith in Your goodness that obeying Your commands and directives is never even a question for me. Enable me to live in obedience. "Make me walk in the path of Your commandments, for I delight in it" (Psalm 119:35).

No temptation has overtaken you except such as is common to man; but God is faithful, who will not allow you to be tempted beyond what you are able, but with the temptation will also make the way of escape, that you may be able to bear it.

1 CORINTHIANS 10:13

Prayer Notes

When I Am Attacked by the Enemy

— ❧ —

Lord, I praise You as my Deliverer and thank You that You will deliver me from my enemies. I know that "we do not wrestle against flesh and blood, but against principalities, against powers, against the rulers of the darkness of this age, against spiritual hosts of wickedness in the heavenly places" (Ephesians 6:12). You will lift me up above those who rise against me and deliver me from the violent forces that oppose me. "Lead me, O LORD, in Your righteousness because of my enemies; make Your way straight before my face" (Psalm 5:8). I give thanks to You, Lord, and sing praises to Your name (Psalm 18:49). Thank You that You always lead us in triumph in Christ (2 Corinthians 2:14).

———— ❧ ————

"No weapon formed against you shall prosper, and every tongue which rises against you in judgment you shall condemn. This is the heritage of the servants of the LORD, and their righteousness is from Me," says the LORD.

ISAIAH 54:17

———— ❧ ————

Prayer Notes

_____

_____

_____

_____

_____

_____

_____

_____

_____

When I Am Attacked
by the Enemy

—— ❧ ——

Lord, I worship You as Lord over everything. I praise You as my all-powerful King. You, Lord, You are "a shield to all who trust" in You (Psalm 18:28-30). You deliver me from the enemy who is too strong for me (Psalm 18:17). I will "not be afraid nor dismayed" because of the force of evil that comes against me, for I know that the battle is not mine but Yours. I know that I will not need to fight this battle alone. Instead, I will position myself in a stance of praise and worship toward You, and I will stand still and see Your salvation, for You are with me (2 Chronicles 20:15-17).

Be strong in the Lord and in the power of His might. Put on the whole armor of God, that you may be able to stand against the wiles of the devil.

EPHESIANS 6:10-11

Prayer Notes

_____

_____

_____

_____

_____

_____

_____

_____

_____

When I Suffer Great Loss, Disappointment, or Failure

— ✣ —

I praise You and worship You, Lord. I love You and recognize that all I have is from You. Everything I have is Yours, and I surrender it all to You for Your glory. Therefore, whatever I have lost I release into Your hands. I praise You and thank You that this is the day that You have made, and I will rejoice and be glad in it. Thank You for Your grace and mercy. Thank You that You love me the way You do. Thank You that You will bring good out of my situation. No matter what has happened or will happen in my life, as long as I am alive I will sing praises to You (Psalm 146:1-2).

These things I have spoken to you, that in Me you may have peace. In the world you will have tribulation; but be of good cheer, I have overcome the world.

JOHN 16:33

Prayer Notes

_____

_____

_____

_____

_____

_____

_____

_____

_____

When I Suffer Great Loss, Disappointment, or Failure

—————— ❧ ——————

O God, You are Lord over heaven and on earth and Lord over my life. I praise You, my precious Redeemer and King. I thank You that You are a God of redemption and restoration. I surrender to You all my grief or sadness over any loss, disappointment, or failure I have experienced and praise You in the midst of it. I thank You, Holy Spirit, that You are my Comforter. Lord, I thank You that You allow no suffering that is without purpose. I know that You are a good God and what You allow will be used for good. I draw close to You in praise and worship, and put my hope in You, for with You there is mercy and redemption (Psalm 130:7).

You number my wanderings; put my tears into Your bottle; are they not in Your book? When I cry out to You, then my enemies will turn back; this I know, because God is for me.

PSALM 56:8-9

Prayer Notes

When I Sense that All Is Well

———— ❧ ————

Lord, I want to show my love for You every day by embracing You with my worship and touching You with my praise. Teach me all I need to know about how to worship You in ways that are pleasing in Your sight. Fill my heart with such great knowledge of You that praising You becomes a way of life. Teach me to make praise my first reaction to every situation, no matter what the situation is. All honor, glory, and majesty belong to You, Lord, for You are worthy to be praised. You are holy and righteous, and I have no greater joy in life than entering into Your presence to exalt You with worship and praise every day.

As you have therefore received Christ Jesus the Lord, so walk in Him, rooted and built up in Him and established in the faith, as you have been taught, abounding in it with thanksgiving.

COLOSSIANS 2:6-7

Prayer Notes

_____

_____

_____

_____

_____

_____

_____

_____

_____

When I Sense that All Is Well

Lord, I worship You for all that You are. You are my Lord in the good times as well as the difficult. On the mountaintop as well as in the valley. I praise You in times of great blessing as well as in times of great challenge. It is because of You that I can stand strong, even when I feel weak. For I know that when I am weakest, You show Yourself strong. I am grateful for Your salvation, deliverance, protection, goodness, and blessings in my life every day. I know that everything I have comes from You. Because of Your great strength I go from glory to glory and "strength to strength" no matter what is happening in my life (Psalm 84:7).

———— ❧ ————

Blessed is everyone who fears the LORD, who walks in His ways. When you eat the labor of your hands, you shall be happy, and it shall be well with you.

PSALM 128:1-2

———— ❧ ————

Prayer Notes

_____

_____

_____

_____

_____

_____

_____

_____

_____

OTHER BOOKS
BY STORMIE OMARTIAN

The Prayer That Changes Everything®

Bestselling author Stormie Omartian shares personal stories, biblical truths, and practical guiding principles to reveal the wonders that take place when Christians offer praise in the middle of difficulties, sorrow, fear, and, yes, abundance and joy.

The Power of a Praying® Woman

Stormie Omartian's bestselling books have helped hundreds of thousands of individuals pray more effectively for their spouses, their children, and their nation. Now she has written a book on a subject she knows intimately: being a praying woman. Stormie's deep knowledge of Scripture and candid examples from her own prayer life provide guidance for women who seek to trust God with deep longings and cover every area of life with prayer.

The Power of a Praying® Wife

Stormie shares how wives can develop a deeper relationship with their husbands by praying for them. With this practical advice on praying for specific areas, including decision-making, fears, spiritual strength, and sexuality, women will discover the fulfilling marriage God intended.

The Power of a Praying® Parent

This powerful book for parents offers 30 easy-to-read chapters that focus on specific areas of prayers for children. This personal, practical guide leads the way to enriched, strong prayer lives for both moms and dads.

Just Enough Light for the Step I'm On

New Christians and those experiencing life changes or difficult times will appreciate Stormie's honesty, candor, and advice based on experience and the Word of God in this collection of devotional readings perfect for the pressures of today's world.